Whoogles

Can a Dog Make a Woman Pregnant?

. . . and Hundreds of Other
Searches That Make You Ask
"Who Would Google That?"

Kendall Almerico and Tess Hottenroth

Avon, Massachusetts

Copyright © 2010 by Kendall Almerico and Tess Hottenroth
All rights reserved.
This book, or parts thereof, may not be reproduced in any
form without permission from the publisher; exceptions are
made for brief excerpts used in published reviews.

Published by
Adams Media, a division of F+W Media, Inc.
57 Littlefield Street, Avon, MA 02322. U.S.A.
www.adamsmedia.com

ISBN 10: 1-4405-1086-5
ISBN 13: 978-1-4405-1086-1
eISBN 10: 1-4405-1111-X
eISBN 13: 978-1-4405-1111-0

Printed in the United States of America.

10   9   8   7   6   5   4   3   2

Library of Congress Cataloging-in-Publication Data
is available from the publisher.

This publication is designed to provide accurate and authoritative information with regard to the subject matter covered. It is sold with the understanding that the publisher is not engaged in rendering legal, accounting, or other professional advice. If legal advice or other expert assistance is required, the services of a competent professional person should be sought.

—From a *Declaration of Principles* jointly adopted by a Committee of the American Bar Association and a Committee of Publishers and Associations

Many of the designations used by manufacturers and sellers to distinguish their product are claimed as trademarks. Where those designations appear in this book and Adams Media was aware of a trademark claim, the designations have been printed with initial capital letters.

This book was not approved, authorized, reviewed, or endorsed by Google Inc., its associates, or affiliates.

This book is available at quantity discounts for bulk purchases.
For information, please call 1-800-289-0963.

Introduction

It all started out very innocently. I was doing research for a book
of memoirs about my years in Africa, and I needed to find out
whether it's possible to cure malaria by drinking copious amounts
of gin and tonic. It was a source of contention among my fellow
expatriates in Nigeria, although I was staunchly in the camp
of those who cite booze with a side of tonic as a panacea for
parasites.

So I did what every person on the planet with access to the
Internet does. I opened my laptop and went to my favorite search
engine, the ultimate authority on everything in the world. No, I did
not go to Wikipedia—I am not that kind of girl. I went to Google.
As I started typing my inquiry, something unexpected happened.
I had only typed the letters "Can I c" when I noticed the box of
results that the Gods of Google so thoughtfully displayed for
me. At the very top of the results, staring at me from my glowing
screen of profound knowledge, was this gem:

Can I catch herpes from my cat?

Huh?

My first thought was, how did this search result end up
on Google? Did some hungover frat boy wake up naked one
afternoon and realize that, despite being the champ of keg stands
while wearing a pink shirt with a popped collar, he had only
managed to bed Tabby from the sorority house? Did he discover

an oozing sore and jump to the conclusion that the wily feline must be the source of this festering blister? And if so, why was his first reaction to ask Google about this appalling revelation? Why not go straight to the campus veterinarian and get some Valtrex?

I called my business consultant and the funniest person I know, Kendall Almerico. After his initial misunderstanding of the conversation and an awkward moment of telling me that venereal diseases resulting from bestiality or my other predilections were slightly outside of the scope of his knowledge, he too began to see the hilarity that resulted from even the most inane questions to the Gods of Google.

We spent the next several hours on the telephone, amazed at what many seemingly innocuous Google searches produced. Not only could we not stop laughing, but we sat with our mouths wide open in utter shock at the indisputable idiocy of a good number of Internet users. In order to show up in these searches, somebody must have actually typed these prizes into Google at some point. The pervasiveness of searches regarding pregnancy, bowel movements, and alarming body odors could not go overlooked. We started collecting these wonderful morsels of moronity, and wondered out loud: Who Googled that? We said it so many times, we decided to call these nuggets of idiocy "Whoogles."

This book is a collection of our favorites, along with the thoughts that went through one of our heads as we found each one. We hope you enjoy them as much as we do. And, when you start finding these Whoogles yourself, feel free to share them with everyone at our website: *www.whoogles.com*.

And of course, we feel it necessary to put a disclaimer in here also. This collection of Whoogles is culled from real Google searches and real suggestion results. We couldn't make up searches this stupid even if we wanted to. Some of the morons who use Google, and thus have afforded us with the opportunity to laugh at the generalized stupidity of members of our society, are idiots whose views we do not share. Google is free and open to all people, except for the Chinese, but we will just leave that out of this for now. If it were not, we would be doing something other than writing this book. Our disagreement with their various points of view does not prevent us from enjoying some fodder and commenting on their stupidity.

This book is not owned by, affiliated with, or approved by Google. It should be, however, since we fully expect that this book and our website is going to drive up the number of Google searches as people try to find more of these hidden gems. As a result, Google is going to make a lot more money. (Note to Google: we expect a nice "thank you" and an annual Christmas card from here on out.) Maybe we should go online and type in "How can I get Google to pay me for driving more traffic to them?" Unfortunately, if we do that, one of the Whoogles will probably be "How can I get George Clooney to enjoy an enema?"

—Tess Hottenroth

Google

how dr
how drugs affect the brain
how drunk am i
how dry cleaning works
how draw cartoons
how dreams work
how drugs affect the body
how dry i am
how dry i am lyrics
how drunk are you calculator
how drugs affect your life

[Google Search] [I'm Feeling Lucky]

If you are asking Google to determine your level of sobriety, please stay out of your vehicle. Last time we checked, Google had not yet implemented the G-breathalyzer feature. But don't worry, there will be an app for that soon.

Google

cats and their p
cats and their **personalities**
cats and their **period**
cats and their **personality**
cats and their **personal stereos**
cats and their **poets**
types of cats and their **personalities**

Google Search   I'm Feeling Lucky

There is nothing more annoying than those freaking felines who refuse to turn down their ghetto blasters to an acceptable level.

Google

```
do z
do zombies exist
do zebras make noise
do zombies poop
do zebras eat meat
do zombies sleep
do zebras migrate
do zoos harm animals
do zebras have striped skin
do zooplankton eat phytoplankton
do zac and vanessa live together
```

Google Search   I'm Feeling Lucky

Of course. We assume from the groans and the fact that most of them come wrapped in double ply Charmin that zombies are, in fact, not really monsters, but rather just sad victims of explosive diarrhea.

Google

```
why am i v|
why am i vomiting
why am i vitamin d deficiency
why am i vomiting blood
why am i vomiting bile
why am i vomiting so much
why am i vomiting yellow
why am i vegetarian
why am i verbally abusive
why am i violent
why am i vomiting foam
```

Google Search   I'm Feeling Lucky

Note to self: next time get a rabies shot before Old Yeller goes on the attack.

Google

```
the bed |
the bed song lyrics amanda palmer
the bed is undefiled
the bed restaurant in miami
the bed is on fire with passion and love
the bed that eats people
the bed store
the bed sitting room
the bed is on fire with passionate love
the bed and breakfast inn at la jolla
the bedwetting store
```

Google Search   I'm Feeling Lucky

When little Johnny is scared of the boogeyman hiding in his closet, or the monster under his bed, you can calm his fears by telling him this happy tale. "No Johnny, there is nothing to be scared of. I checked your closet, and I looked under the mattress. Let's just hope you don't have that bed that eats people. Good night. Don't let the bed bugs bite!"

Google

```
can you be c|
can you be charged without being arrested
can you be christian and buddhist
can you be contagious without a fever
can you be claimed as a dependent
can you be caught downloading torrents
can you be constipated and have diarrhea
can you be color blind in one eye
can you be charged with a dui after the fact
can you be convicted without evidence
can you be catholic and pro choice
```

[Google Search] [I'm Feeling Lucky]

This Whoogle leads to other great philosophical conundrums. Can you be blind, and have sight? Can you be deaf, and have hearing? Is the Pope Catholic? Does a bear crap in the woods? What if the bear is constipated? See how we went full circle with that one?

Google

what is it
what is it **like to die**
what is it **called when a word is** spelled the same backwards
what is it **called when a giraffe swallowed a toy jet**
what is it **lyrics**
what is it **called when a change** is made in the constitution
what is it **like to be a bat**
what is it **worth**
what is it **like to be high**
what is it **like to have breasts**
what is it **called when you like pain**

Google Search   I'm Feeling Lucky

It's called a violation of every zoo's simple request that you don't feed the animals.

Google

is it illegal to e|

is it illegal to eat an orange in a bathtub in california
is it illegal to eat dog in america
is it illegal to eat while driving
is it illegal to eat cats
is it illegal to eat a human
is it illegal to email music
is it illegal to eat a dog
is it illegal to eat dog
is it illegal to eat cats in america
is it illegal to eat dolphin

Google Search   I'm Feeling Lucky

Ever since the Governator took over, his number one priority has been enforcing this important piece of legislation that keeps the people of California safe. The Constables of Commode Citrus Consumption have been so effective, that most naval nibblers have moved next door to Nevada, where gambling, prostitution, and shower citrus sucking are seen as revenue sources, not criminal acts.

Google

```
why are t
why are the kardashians famous
why are there school
why are the flags at half mast today
why are there so many earthquakes lately
why are they called killer whales
why are tigers endangered
why are the linked rings an olympic symbol
why are there no cats in the bible
why are there no earthquakes in florida
why are there strawberries on my
```

[Google Search]   [I'm Feeling Lucky]

There are three great mysteries in the universe. Number One is Stonehenge. Number Two is "Why do men have nipples?" This Whoogle is Number Three.

Google

why cant dogs s
why cant dogs see in color
why cant dogs see tv
why cant dogs speak english
why cant dogs smile
why cant dogs speak

[Google Search] [I'm Feeling Lucky]

Most dogs can speak English, but simply choose not to. Chihuahuas, on the other hand, only speak Mexican. Likewise, Poodles only speak French. This is elementary stuff you could glean from any Disney film; it's not rocket science. If your owner was constantly telling you in a weird baby voice to sit, stay, roll over, and play dead, your desire to intelligently communicate with humans would be severely diminished also.

Google

```
flossd
floss daily
flossdental.com
flossdaily darth vader
flosstradamus
flossdaily before you read this
flossdaily sterile
```

[Google Search] [I'm Feeling Lucky]

One can only imagine the horrific state of dental health that must ensue when you wear a black helmet twenty-four hours a day. And just to be sure we were not missing anything, we watched all six Star Wars movies again, and we're quite certain that not one character ever brushed their teeth or visited a dentist, despite fan mail that must have poured in from even the most avid fans requesting that Jabba the Hut get some lessons in oral hygiene. And, despite claims by Lucasfilms to the contrary, Jar Jar Binks did not receive a dental degree from the University of Tatooine.

Google

```
does mo|
does mountain dew lower sperm count
does morality depend on religion
does monistat 7 work
does mountain dew shrink testicles
does mobile im use internet
does morgan freeman have children
does mountain dew kill sperm
does money buy happiness
does mountain dew make you smaller
does morning sickness come and go
```

Google Search   I'm Feeling Lucky

Yes! And douching with Mr. Pibb right after sex prevents conception. Spraying Fanta all over your tits makes them bigger. Soft drinks are great for all kinds of unknown medico-sexual purposes.

Google

is it ok to eat expired |

is it ok to eat expired **yogurt**
is it ok to eat expired **eggs**
is it ok to eat expired **canned food**
is it ok to eat expired **popcorn**
is it ok to eat expired **peanut butter**
is it ok to eat expired **chocolate**
is it ok to eat expired **vitamins**
is it ok to eat expired **bread**
is it ok to eat expired **food**
is it ok to eat expired **jello**

Google Search   I'm Feeling Lucky

Yes, it is fine. However, you may as well start asking Google, "Why am I projectile vomiting" now.

Google

```
police horses for
police horses for sale
police horses for adoption
police horses for sale san diego
police horses for auction
police horses for rehoming
police horses for sale uk
police horses for loan
```

[Google Search] [I'm Feeling Lucky]

Obvious next question, are there laws against galloping through the streets on these trusty steeds whilst I am intoxicated? If not, sign me up. Seriously, how cool would it be to walk out of the bar after last call and, while everybody else is making futile attempts at hailing a cab, to saddle up my loaner Secretariat to canter my drunk ass home? Now that I am thinking about things I would like to borrow from the cops, I would also like to know if I can get a discount lease on a Taser and some handcuffs for the evening?

Google

```
birth in a |
```

birth in a **box**
birth in a **bathtub**
birth in a **car**
birth in a **squatting position**
birth in a **hammock**
birth in a **hospital**
birth in a **pool**
birth in a **caul**
birth in a **tree**

| Google Search | I'm Feeling Lucky |

The newest trend in "going green." Look for Arbor Lamaze classes at a hospital near you.

Google

```
do home
do homemade ouija boards work
do home drug tests work
do home security systems work
do homeopathic remedies work
do homework for me
do homework online
do homework
do homeless people choose to be homeless
do homeschoolers get into college
do home electrolysis kits work
```

[Google Search] [I'm Feeling Lucky]

Yes. Studies have proven that they are 100 percent as reliable as the boards sold by Parker Brothers.

Google

I didn't know I |

i didn't know i **was pregnant**
i didn't know i **was pregnant episodes**
i didn't know i **was pregnant stories**
i didn't know i **was pregnant tlc**
i didn't know i **was pregnant episodes online**
i didn't know i **was pregnant and drank alcohol**
i didn't know i **was pregnant wiki**
i didn't know i **had to take a dump**
i didn't know i **had to take a dump the soup**
i didn't know i **was pregnant toilet**

Google Search | I'm Feeling Lucky

This was just in Sunday's Home Depot ad. Apparently, as you urinate, the toilet turns blue and is covered with little plus signs if you are, in fact, with child. Either that or this is the commode for women who go through nine months of having no clue that they are pregnant and are all over the news in a state of total shock when they suddenly crap out a chitlin.

Google

```
does a ti
    does a tiger wear a necktie
    does a tiger wear a necktie monologue
    does a tilted uterus affect fertility
    does a title of a book need to be underlined
    does a tiger wear a necktie script
    does a timing chain need to be replaced
    does a tilted uterus affect pregnancy
    does a tiger have striped skin
    does a time machine exist
    does a tia show up on an mri

              Google Search    I'm Feeling Lucky
```

He used to, especially when attending a business meeting. But not anymore, since he is understandably concerned about having anything noose-like already around his neck when Elin is in close proximity.

chances of getting caught s
chances of getting caught **shoplifting**
chances of getting caught **selling drugs**

Google Search   I'm Feeling Lucky

Around 100 percent if you are stupid enough to ask Google what your chances are of getting caught shoplifting rather than a more salient question like, "What can I do to prevent getting caught shoplifting?"

Google

```
do b|
do better lyrics say anything
do black people get sunburnt
do blind people dream
do better lyrics
do bananas cause constipation
do babies poop in the womb
do braces hurt
do bats hibernate
do bees have knees
do bananas have seeds
```

[Google Search] [I'm Feeling Lucky]

Some babies in utero are potty trained enough to get to the womb port-o-let that is physiologically generated during the average human pregnancy. It is found just outside the womb, right next to the spleen.

Google

can pigs e
can pigs eat **humans**
can pigs eat **chocolate**
can pigs eat **meat**
can pigs eat **bones**
can pigs eat **bacon**
can pigs eat **hay**
can pigs eat **pork**
can pigs eat **acorns**
can pigs eat **people**
can pigs eat **chicken bones**

[Google Search] [I'm Feeling Lucky]

Not Kosher pigs.

Google

```
why am i tr|
```

why am i **trying to live when i'm just living to die lyrics**
why am i **treated so bad lyrics**
why am i **treated so bad**
why am i **transgendered**
why am i **trembling**
why am i **trying to give when no one gives me a try lyrics**
why am i **trying to become what i don't want to be**
why am i **tired all the time**
why am i **trying to live if i'm just living to die lyrics**
why am i **trustworthy**

Google Search   I'm Feeling Lucky

Isn't it a bit late to be asking this question? This thought should have been processed before you jetted off to see Dr. Sven and underwent that procedure in Stockholm to turn Willie into Wilma.

Google

```
i am di|
i am disappoint
i am dina
i am disinclined to acquiesce to your request
i am disappoint original
i am diddy
i am diddy twitter
i am different quotes
i am discourses
i am dizzy
i am disappointment in you're grammar
```

Google Search | I'm Feeling Lucky

I am much less disappointment, and even somewhat surprised, that this idiot knew how to correctly spell grammar.

Google

```
can you buy |
can you buy lottery tickets with a credit card
can you buy liquor online
can you buy lottery tickets online
can you buy land on the moon
can you buy lemon zest
can you buy liquid nitrogen
can you buy life insurance on someone else
can you buy laughing gas
can you buy liquor in utah
can you buy land in hawaii
```

[Google Search] [I'm Feeling Lucky]

Yes. Just send $10,000 per acre (or whatever you can afford) to the authors of this book for your own plot of lunar land. And while you are at it, could you fly to Nigeria and pick up a suitcase with $35 million in cash from my friend whose husband was jailed? She just needs someone to go over there and bring her $2,000 cash so she can pay for the key to the safe deposit box.

Google

i love to w

i love to wear diapers
i love to worship you lyrics
i love to watch a woman dance lyrics
i love to watch
i love to watch a woman dance
i love to watch her strut
i love to write
i love to watch her leave lyrics
i love to walk in the rain lyrics
i love to watch her leave

Google Search | I'm Feeling Lucky

Depends 4 Ever!

Google

pre|

preakness stakes 2010
pregnancy week by week
preakness
pregnancy calculator
prednisone
precious
pregnancy symptoms
pregnancy
prednisone side effects
pregnancy pact

[Google Search] [I'm Feeling Lucky]

Hewlett Packard's finest invention. 1 penis + 1 vagina + 1,000,000 sperm - 1 birth control device = 1 fetus.

Google

```
are chickens
are chickens mammals
are chickens smart
are chickens asexual
are chickens cold blooded
are chickens male or female
are chickens birds
are chickens color blind
are chickens dinosaurs
are chickens good pets
are chickens related to dinosaurs
```

Google Search   I'm Feeling Lucky

Yes, Virginia. Chickens are dinosaurs. And turkeys are cavemen. So hop on over to KFC and get a bucket of brontosaurus. As for that drumstick? You got it. It's from a pterodactyl.

Google

```
sometimes i wonder|
sometimes i wonder lyrics
sometimes i wonder why is that frisbee getting bigger and then it hit me
sometimes i wonder quotes
sometimes i wonder how i keep from going under
sometimes i wonder who i am
sometimes i wonder who you'd be today lyrics
sometimes i wonder where i've been
sometimes i wonder why you even love me
sometimes i wonder why
sometimes i wonder goodfellas
```

[Google Search] [I'm Feeling Lucky]

In order to avoid expensive litigation, Wham-O needs to add a warning label that reads: Attention uncoordinated pothead. The plastic disc your stoner buddy hurled at you may be closer than it appears.

Google

is it a good idea to microwave a

is it a good idea to microwave an **airbag**
is it a good idea to microwave an **electric blanket**
is it a good idea to microwave a **large firework**
is it a good idea to microwave a **bottle rocket**
is it a good idea to microwave a microwave
is it a good idea to microwave a **match**
is it a good idea to microwave an **ipod**
is it a good idea to microwave an **icy penguin**
is it a good idea to microwave a **television**
is it a good idea to microwave a **cat**

Google Search   I'm Feeling Lucky

Good idea? Probably not. But, sometimes when Tabby goes out in the rain, a good old-fashioned towel drying is just too time consuming in today's busy world. Lure Tabby into the microwave with some catnip, close the door, and push the Popcorn setting. Rest assured you will never have to dry off your feline friend again.

Google

where did i p

where did i **put my keys**

where did i **put my weed**

where did i **put my ipod**

where did i **put my wallet**

where did i **park iphone app**

where did i **put my phone**

where did i **put my cell phone**

where did i **put my glasses**

where did i **park my car app**

where did i **put the remote**

[Google Search] [I'm Feeling Lucky]

Dude. Seriously. And where in the hell are my Funyuns?

Google

is j

is **justin bieber bi**
is **justin bieber a virgin**
is **justin bieber dead**
is **johnny depp dead**
is **jillian michaels straight**
is **justin bieber single**
is **jailbreaking illegal**
is **justin bieber dating selena gomez**
is **justin bieber a christian**
is **jamie lee curtis a hermaphrodite**

Google Search | I'm Feeling Lucky

No. The guards in jails and prisons actually generally encourage convicts to go Shawshank-style from time to time. It might save some tax dollars and help to balance the budget if all those annoying criminals would quit taking advantage of free rent and move out sooner rather than later.

Google

```
why
why can't i own a canadian
why is my poop green
why is a raven like a writing desk
why is the sky blue
why do dogs eat poop
why are people posting colors on facebook
why did i get married too
why dont we just dance lyrics
why did the chicken cross the road
why do cats purr
```

[Google Search] [I'm Feeling Lucky]

Check your rectal calendar. It's St. Patrick's Day in your ass! Erin Go Bragh! If this is truly a problem, the correct search inquiry should be "gastrointestinal physician near me." Then, you should get some Lysol and disinfect your keyboard before somebody catches that green shit.

Google

did my water brea
did my water break
did my water break or did i pee
did my water break or did i pee my pants
did my water break did pee my pants
why did my water break early
did i pee or did my water break

Google Search   I'm Feeling Lucky

Maybe you should work on getting your sogginess all cleaned up and getting yourself to the delivery ward instead of wasting your time asking Google to figure out what fluids are gushing out of you and ruining that shag carpet you should have replaced in 1979.

Google

```
bacon d|
bacon dressing for spinach salad
bacon donut
bacon dressing
bacon double cheddar crisp
bacon dip
bacon dessert recipes
bacon davis prevailing wage
bacon dip recipe
bacon diet
bacon doughnut
```

[Google Search] [I'm Feeling Lucky]

This sounds like something you get at one of those contemporary trendy restaurants that can't seem to put together a dish with anything fewer than thirty ingredients in a combination that has never been tried before, albeit for good reason. I don't want hot fudge sauce on my steak. Save the chocolate bits as a topping for my ice cream, not the Bac-Os.

Google

```
can you pee |
can you pee with a tampon in
can you pee while wearing a tampon
can you pee with a tampon in you
can you pee and poop at the same time
can you pee out fat
can you pee out a baby
can you pee out a miscarriage
can you pee on a pregnancy test twice
can you pee on a jellyfish sting
can you pee after using monistat
```

        [Google Search] [I'm Feeling Lucky]

Tired of conventional calorie counting and exercise? Sick of figuring out the grams of carbs or the Weight Watcher points? Who needs those crazy fad methods of losing weight? Just drink a lot of water, then urinate out that nasty fat and flush it down the toilet! Why didn't I think of that before?

Google

i want to ha

i want to have **a baby**
i want to have **twins**
i want to have **an affair**
i want to have **a miscarriage**
i want to have **intercourse with you**
i want to have **a baby girl**
i want to have **a baby boy**
i want to have **your babies lyrics**
i want to have **your abortion**
i want to have **a baby but i'm single**

Google Search   I'm Feeling Lucky

Yeah you, Google. You sexy bitch, you. You know my secrets, my fears, my questions, and you have the answers, you comfort me when I am lonely or afraid. It is definitely time to take our relationship to the next level.

Google

---

never let a c

never let a **crisis go to waste**

never let a **crackhead sing** at **your funeral**

never let a **crisis go to waste quote**

never let a **crackhead sing at your wedding**

never let a **crisis**

never let a **cowboy make the coffee**

never let a **crackhead sing** at a **funeral**

never let a **crisis go**

never let a **chance go by**

never let a **chance go by oh lord**

Google Search | I'm Feeling Lucky

True words of priceless wisdom.

Google

```
why cant he
```

| why cant he **get hard** |
| why cant he **be you lyrics** |
| why cant he **get it up** |
| why cant he**len keller drive** |
| why cant he **stay hard** |
| why cant he **keep it up** |
| why cant he **love me** |
| why cant he **commit** |
| why cant he **say i love you** |
| why **can her**pes **be cured** |

[Google Search] [I'm Feeling Lucky]

It probably has something to do with the fact that you are the type of person who pours your relationship problems out to Google.

Google

```
can i catch her
can i catch herpes from kissing
can i catch herpes from my partner
can i catch herpes from a toilet
can i catch herpes from touching
can i catch herpes from a toilet seat
can i catch herpes from my cat
can i catch herpes from a towel
can i catch herpes from a cold sore
can i catch herpes in a hot tub
can i catch herpes from my friend
```

Google Search   I'm Feeling Lucky

I hate it when my cat seduces me and leaves me the next morning with a little present that reminds me of my feline indiscretion for the rest of my life.

Google

can you be fired for b

can you be fired for **being sick**
can you be fired for **being pregnant**
can you be fired for **being arrested**
can you be fired for **being depressed**
can you be fired for **bad credit**
can you be fired for **bad weather**
can you be fired for **being late**
can you be fired for **bankruptcy**
can you be fired for **being an alcoholic**
can you be fired for **being on disability**

Google Search | I'm Feeling Lucky

Unless your job title is "Sun," "Rain," or "Mother Nature," I am guessing probably not.

Google

```
can you m|
can you meet me halfway lyrics
can you microwave styrofoam
can you milk a hamster
can you mix breast milk with formula
can you make money on youtube
can you mail a gun
can you make soap without lye
can you mail cigarettes
can you move out at 17 in florida
can you miss a period and not be pregnant
```

Google Search   I'm Feeling Lucky

Of course. You can milk anything with nipples. However, to get enough hamster milk to dunk your Oreos in, you will need to let the little rats multiply like rabbits first. Do rabbits have nipples?

Google

```
why wont my p
```

why wont my **parakeet eat** my **diarrhea**
why wont my **parrot eat** my **diarrhea**
why wont my **puppy eat**
why wont my **printer print**
why wont my **ps3 connect to the internet**
why wont my **ps3 work on** my **tv**
why wont my **ps3 read discs**
why wont my **phone charge**
why wont my **period stop**
why wont my **ps3 play ps2 games**

Google Search | I'm Feeling Lucky

Parakeets are notoriously picky eaters, so getting those annoying mini-parrots to eat properly is very difficult. Experts suggest disguising your diarrhea as something else. Mix it with chocolate or cover it with powdered sugar. If that does not work, guilt the little bird into eating it by telling him there are starving children out there who would love to eat your diarrhea.

Google

jesus playing h
jesus playing h**ockey**

[Google Search] [I'm Feeling Lucky]

Didn't you know that Jesus was the NHL (National Hebrew League) MVP in 29 A.D., coincidentally, when he was twenty-nine years old? Little known fact: Jesus invented the slap shot while scoring his 100th goal for the Jerusalem Jews in the Stanley Cup final that year.

Google

```
can you aff|
```
can you afford **to retire**
can you afford **a house calculator**
can you afford **a house**
can you afford **fries with that**
can you afford **to be a stay at home mom**
can you afford **a baby**
can you afford **it suze orman**
can you afford **to move out**
can you afford **to stay home**
can you afford **a car**

[Google Search] [I'm Feeling Lucky]

There is nothing more irritating than when the smart ass fifteen-
year-old kid at Mickey D's mocks your earning capacity when
you ask for your favorite fried spud side dish to accompany your
heart stopping grease burger. Generally, my response is, "Can you
afford some acne cream? Apparently not."

Google

```
do old p
```

| do old **people have grey pubic hair** |
| do old **people eat cat food** |
| do old **people shrink** |
| do old **people have pubic hair** |
| do old **people smell** |
| do old **people fear death** |
| do old **people need less sleep** |
| do old **people sleep more** |
| do old **people like eat** |
| do old **people get swine flu** |

[Google Search]   [I'm Feeling Lucky]

Only when the kind nurses at the nursing home feed them. So, no.

Google

```
why do i hav|
why do i have so much discharge
why do i have no friends
why do i have four nipples
why do i have so much gas
why do i have to pee so much
why do i have diarrhea
why do i have gas all the time
why do i have nightmares
why do i have dandruff
why do i have bags under my eyes
```

[Google Search] [I'm Feeling Lucky]

Is this honestly a question you feel would be addressed better by some teenage blogger on Wikipedia rather than consulting a real doctor? Or even a pseudo doctor, the kind that you see in the emergency room that looks like an even younger version of Doogie Howser who got his medical degree through a correspondence course while paying for his course load by running the corner lemonade stand? Come to think of it, maybe the teenage blogger would be better. . . .

Google

```
are pir|
```

are piranhas legal in florida
are pirates real
are piranhas illegal
are piranhas endangered
are pirelli tires good
are piranhas dangerous
are piranhas freshwater fish
are pirates still around
are pirates better than ninjas
are piranhas edible

[Google Search] [I'm Feeling Lucky]

This obviously depends completely on the pirate and the ninja in question. Johnny Depp is better than the Teenage Mutant Ninja Turtles, except maybe Raphael who might be able to kick Jack Sparrow's ass in hand to turtle hand combat. Jackie Chan, on the other hand, could take Black Beard any day on any ship.

Google

is it wrong to sleep with
is it wrong to sleep with **your sister**
is it wrong to sleep with **your cousin**
is it wrong to sleep with **your dog**
is it wrong to sleep with **your brother**
is it wrong to sleep with **your dad**
is it wrong to sleep with **your mom**
is it wrong to sleep with **your aunt**
is it wrong to sleep with **a married woman**
is it wrong to sleep with **your second cousin**
is it wrong to sleep with **your step brother**

Google Search   I'm Feeling Lucky

You really have to look down this list. Is it wrong to sleep with your sister? Your brother? Your cousin? Your dad? Your mom? Your aunt? Your dog? I am going to petition Google to reprogram their algorithm so that "Is it weird that my kids have serious psychological issues" is included as the next logical search suggestion here.

Google

god j

god jokes
god john lennon lyrics
god john lennon
god jupiter
god journey
god jesus robot
god janus
god jul
god jesus and the holy spirit
god judges the heart

Google Search   I'm Feeling Lucky

The not-so-holy trinity. Just picture how mass might start, "in the name of the father, and the son and the Holy C-3PO"

Google

can monk
can monk**eys swim**
can monk**eys talk**
can monk**eys cry**
can monk**s marry**
can monk**eys be pets**
can monk**eys fly**
can monk**eys smoke weed**
can monk**eys get aids**
can monk**eys laugh**
can monk**eys and humans mate**

[Google Search] [I'm Feeling Lucky]

I didn't think it was possible until I saw an old television show from when the Olsen twins were little. Hmmm. . . .

Google

```
can i pus|
can i push a hemorrhoid back in
can i push your stool in
can i push my piles back in
```

[Google Search] [I'm Feeling Lucky]

Yes, but be sure to wash your hands with soap thoroughly after you do. You have no idea where that hemorrhoid has been.

Google

is my kid |

is my kid **smoking pot**

is my kid **on drugs**

is my kid **ready for kindergarten**

is my kid **autistic**

is my kid **overweight**

is my kid **emo**

is my kid **gifted**

is my kid **a genius**

is my kid **color blind**

is my kid **adhd**

Google Search   I'm Feeling Lucky

Can you use Johnny Jr.'s belt to measure the equator? Did little Sally have to get her baby pictures taken by satellite? When your boy runs from across the yard does he influence the tides? If the answer to any of the above is "Yes," then your child is officially a fatty.

Google

```
can i s
can i substitute butter for shortening
can i still have a period and be pregnant
can i start a sentence with because
can i stay lyrics
can i stay ray lamontagne lyrics
can i sell my iphone
can i sell my kidney
can i send a fax from my computer
can i sing
```

Google Search   I'm Feeling Lucky

I am pretty sure there is a group in New Jersey that has cornered the market and is still buying them for about $7 per kidney. Oh scratch that. They seem to have been arrested. Better luck in Iran.

Google

i like to k|

i like to **keep this handy achievement**
i like to **kill flies**
i like to **kill deer ringtone**
i like to **kill deer**
i like to **keep this handy for close encounters**
i like to **kick stretch and kick**
i like to **keep this for close encounters**
i like to **keep this handy**
i like to **know lyrics**
i like to **kick guys in the balls**

Google Search   I'm Feeling Lucky

In related news, I am still single.

Google

why do my|
why do my **breasts hurt**
why do my **balls smell**
why do my **nipples itch**
why do my **ears ring**
why do my **balls hurt**
why do my **legs itch when i run**
why do my **hands shake**
why do my **breasts itch**
why do my **bones crack**
why do my **ears hurt when i run**

Google Search   I'm Feeling Lucky

Because that shockingly single girl kicked them.

Google

| smack a t |
| smack a **twilight fan day** |
| smack a **thief** |
| smack a **troll** |

Google Search   I'm Feeling Lucky

I must say I was a little distressed by this one because of the
obvious implication that I am not permitted to smack Twilight fans
on the other 364¼ days of the year. I think we should come up
with a few more of these holidays. Immediately coming to mind are
"bite a vampire day" and "stake your least favorite werewolf day."

Google

```
is bull|
```

is bullying a crime
is bullfighting a sport
is bully beatdown real
is bullying illegal
is bully beatdown staged
is bullet for my valentine emo
is bullying against the law
is bully a good game
is bull sperm in red bull
is bully beatdown scripted

[Google Search] [I'm Feeling Lucky]

Yes. Red Bull is expensive because the matadors charge an arm and a leg and a ball for each one of those precious drops of bull semen. The next time you need an energy burst, just remember that you would get a bigger adrenaline rush and be out of pocket less money if you collected some bull sperm yourself.

Google

```
how to roll a j
how to roll a joint
how to roll a joint with a dollar
how to roll a joint without rolling paper
how to roll a joint step by step
how to roll a joint video
how to roll a joint with a cigarette
how to roll a joint with regular paper
how to roll a joint with bible paper
how to roll a jelly roll
how to roll a joint with zig zags
```

[Google Search]   [I'm Feeling Lucky]

I have forgotten a few of my Sunday School lessons over the last couple of years, but I am pretty sure that there is an explicit commandment regarding this. Thou Shalt Not Use the Word of God in Thy Quest to Get High. Or something along those lines. If you must break this commandment, be sure to use a Gideon's Bible from the sleaziest motel you can find on the roadside just to be certain that the good book has probably already been used for something more sacrilegious than your attempt to smoke enough weed to cavort with the angels.

Google

```
is it illegal to fo
is it illegal to follow someone
is it illegal to follow someone in a car
is it illegal to forge a signature
is it illegal to follow a cop
is it illegal to forward an email
is it illegal to forge a doctor's note
is it illegal to follow an ambulance
```

[Google Search] [I'm Feeling Lucky]

Yes. Next time you think about clicking the "send" button and I am on your spam list as you forward the cute pictures of fuzzy animals and a warning at the end that my soul will be in mortal peril if I do not immediately send it back to you and to 500 of my closest friends, please be aware that I will be filing a police report along with a recommendation that you be punished to the maximum extent allowed by law. For those of you who are not aware, this punishment means sitting in a cubicle for a week and doing nothing but reading the bullshit you have sent to me over the past five years.

Google

does the g|

does the **government owe me money**
does the **government lie to us**
does the **government know about 2012**
does the **gazelle work**
does the **grapefruit diet work**
does the **government monitor** the **internet**
does the **grapefruit diet really work**
does the **glee cast actually sing**
does the **guy die in dear john**
does the **government monitor text messages**

Google Search   I'm Feeling Lucky

Short answer, no. The government is so bankrupt as a result of spending your hard earned tax dollars on health care reform and bank and motor bailouts that they can no longer afford calendars to make them aware that there will be yet another new year in a few short months. They can't even afford the pinups of ravishingly handsome cabana boys posing provocatively in bathroom stalls.

Google

```
is it bad to |
is it bad to crack your knuckles
is it bad to sleep with a bra on
is it bad to crack your back
is it bad to wash your hair everyday
is it bad to manually force poop out of your body
is it bad to crack your neck
is it bad to swallow gum
is it bad to eat late at night
is it bad to run everyday
is it bad to drink too much water
```

[Google Search] [I'm Feeling Lucky]

Everyday people around the world are passing on laxatives, bran cereal, Metamucil, and even a good old-fashioned enema in favor of the manual method of defecation. Look for do-it-yourself products to make the task even easier, coming soon to an infomercial near you. Don't like the mess? Tired of the hassle of shoving your own hand up your ass to man handle those stubborn turds? Now, there's the Colon Poop Scoop! Bye-bye icky hands, hello handle! But wait, there's more! If you order in the next ten minutes, we will throw in the Popeil Pocket Catheter Kit for Free! Never manually urinate again!

Google

```
can you po
can you pop your cherry with a finger
can you port a number to magicjack
can you pop popcorn with a cell phone
can you pop a cold sore
can you pop herpes
can you pop your cherry with a tampon
can you poop with a tampon in
can you pop a stye
can you pop your cherry more than once
can you powder coat aluminum
```

[Google Search] [I'm Feeling Lucky]

Time for another anatomy lesson from Dr. Whoogles. You know that hole from which you defecate? If you are placing a tampon in there, Susie, well, let's just say, you missed.

Google

i wish i had t
i wish i had **that**
i wish i had **the courage to be an absolute nobody**
i wish i had **the courage to say everything i planned to**
i wish i had **the power the power to change the world**
i wish i had **talent**
i wish i had **the power the power to change the world lyrics**
i wish i had **thought of that**
i wish i had **the courage to die**
i wish i had **three hands**
i wish i had **the words**

Google Search | I'm Feeling Lucky

This is proof positive that Paris Hilton uses Google as her search engine.

Google

```
is it illegal to st
is it illegal to steal wireless internet
is it illegal to stream movies online
is it illegal to stop payment on a check
is it illegal to steal wifi
is it illegal to stream movies
is it illegal to stalk someone
is it illegal to steal street signs
is it illegal to stream tv shows
is it illegal to steal a shopping cart
is it illegal to steal trash
```

[Google Search]   [I'm Feeling Lucky]

Here is a word of advice. If you are asking if it is "illegal" to "steal" anything, you obviously were not taught the meaning of the word "steal."

Google

```
do chr
do christians believe in dinosaurs
do christians celebrate halloween
do christians believe in ghosts
do christians believe in reincarnation
do christians sin
do christians believe in aliens
do christians believe in 2012
do christians believe in evolution
do christians celebrate christmas
do christians believe in karma
```

[Google Search]   [I'm Feeling Lucky]

Obviously they do. While the books of the New Testament are a bit sketchy on Jurassic Era details, most people will remember how Jesus raised Lazarus from the dead, but only after stopping to pull a troublesome thorn out of the foot of Lazarus' pet Triceratops, Pointy.

Google

```
my boyfriend fa
my boyfriend farts too much
my boyfriend farts in front of me
my boyfriend farts all the time
my boyfriend family hates me
my boyfriend farts on me
my boyfriend falls asleep
my boyfriend farts a lot
my boyfriend farts in his sleep
my boyfriend facebook
my boyfriend falling out love me
```

[Google Search] [I'm Feeling Lucky]

If your boyfriend's idea of holding hands is him constantly telling you to pull his finger, it is time to get a new boyfriend.

Google

```
can u t|
```

can u **text** with ipod touch
can u **tan** while pregnant
can u **take** tylenol while pregnant
can u **text 911**
can u **track** a cell phone
can u **take** benadryl while pregnant
can u **text** from a computer
can u **track** an ipod touch
can u **take** a bath while pregnant
can u **tell** who is looking at your facebook

[Google Search] [I'm Feeling Lucky]

Hey 911, FML! OMG accident Tiger Woods LISB. WSOHWGC! CUL8R! Luckily dispatchers have been trained to decode these cryptic information bits. For future reference, the next time you text 911, LISB is short for "laying in street bleeding," WSOHWGC is short for "wife standing over him with golf club."

Google

```
how to make my p
how to make my pennis longer
how to make my pictures move side to side on myspace
how to make my pennis longer naturally
how to make my printer wireless
how to make my pennies bigger
how to make my pc faster
how to make my pc bluetooth compatible
how to make my playlist smaller on myspace
how to make my period start
how to make my period end faster
```

[Google Search] [I'm Feeling Lucky]

The stance of the U.S. government on this issue is fairly clear.
Your pennies are standard size and not meant to be any bigger.
However, if you are really in need of enlarged pennies, feel free
to head to the nearest set of train tracks, put your pennies on the
railway, and wait for the next Amtrak to pass. Remember, size
does not matter. Big or small, it is still only one cent.

Google

```
can fa
can fan
can facebook track visitors
can facebook track views
can fat turn into muscle
can fatty liver be reversed
can factory brooklyn
can farts kill you
can fabes
can farmville animals die
can fan combo
```

[Google Search]   [I'm Feeling Lucky]

Of course they can. Haven't you heard of silent but deadly?

Google

```
can i eat a
can i eat a potato with sprouts
can i eat a hot dog when pregnant
can i eat a potato that has sprouted
can i eat a hot dog while pregnant
can i eat a potato with eyes
can i eat a green potato
can i eat a dead lobster
can i eat a green banana
can i eat a brown avocado
can i eat a whole avocado
```

| Google Search | I'm Feeling Lucky |

Eating a dead lobster is always preferable to eating a live lobster. For one thing, live lobsters tend to poke you in the eyes with their snapping claws as you try to put them into your mouth. And, heaven knows, PETA will be all over your ass if they see you dipping Larry The Lobster into drawn butter while his little crustacean heart is still beating.

Google

```
stalkers
stalkers on facebook
stalkers profile
stalkers anonymous
stalkers definition
stalker.com
stalkers on facebook application
stalkers facebook
stalkers list facebook
stalkers make better lovers lyrics
stalkers quotes
```

[Google Search] [I'm Feeling Lucky]

I am curious now about this. How do the meetings work? Do they all converge in a church basement for cookies and juice to fess up to their penchant for binoculars? Or is it more of a situation where everybody sits in various trees (strategically located, obviously) outside the room and peers through the curtains and in a creepy whisper admits that they are an addict? And how do they stop the attendees from following other attendees home?

Google

```
i just sh
i just shot marvin in the face
i just shot john lennon lyrics
i just sharted
i just shitted a big mac
i just shot john lennon
i just shot a bear
i just showed up for my own life lyrics
i just shocked myself
i just shot an elephant in my pajamas
i just shot bill murray

        Google Search    I'm Feeling Lucky
```

Two all beef patties, special sauce, lettuce, cheese, pickles, onions, and sesame seed bun and all. But for some reason, my colon held the fries and the rest of my supersize meal.

Google

```
can i pul|
can i pull my own tooth
can i pull off red hair
can i pull off bangs
can i pull off blonde hair
can i pull off short hair
can i pull off black hair
can i pull my own wisdom tooth
can i pull off a pixie cut
can i pull off skinny jeans
can i pull off red lipstick
```

[Google Search]   [I'm Feeling Lucky]

Given the idiotic nature of this Whoogle, I seriously doubt you have a "wisdom" anything in your body.

Google

```
can making o|
```
can making out get you pregnant

[Google Search] [I'm Feeling Lucky]

Are there no mandatory health and sex-ed classes in high school anymore? Where are your parents with the birds and the bees discussion? How is it that these kids (God, I hope they are not adults) are literate enough to correctly type that sentence, but not informed enough to know that a sperm and an egg are unlikely to meet on your tongue?

Google

i like to eat c
i like to eat cake while excruciating
i like to eat **cake in a tub**
i like to eat **cheese**
i like to eat **chalk**

[Google Search]   [I'm Feeling Lucky]

Is excruciating no longer an adjective? Also on my list of things to occupy my time while excruciating are playing solitaire and knitting a tunic.

Google

barfing g|

burping games
barfing **gif**
barfing **girl**
barfing **games online**
barfing **game**

[Google Search]   [I'm Feeling Lucky]

The possibilities here are endless. There is the contest to see
who can hold their vomit in their mouth for the longest without
throwing up again. Projectile Mania, whoever blows their chunks
the longest distance gets a mashed up hot dog as their prize. And
of course, Emesis Bingo for the old folks.

Google

where do birds go w
where do birds go **when it rains**
where do birds go **when it snows**
where do birds go **when they die**
where do birds go **when it storms**
where do birds go **when it is cold**
where do birds go **when it's windy**

[Google Search] [I'm Feeling Lucky]

Usually on the large plate glass window in my living room.

Google

why cant i u
why cant i **upload photos on facebook**
why cant i **upload videos on youtube**
why cant i **update my iphone**
why cant i **update my iphone to 4.0**
why cant i **use my flying mount in northrend**
why cant i **upload pictures to facebook**
why cant i **upload videos on facebook**
why cant i **urinate**
why cant i **update itunes**
why cant i **use a tampon**

Google Search   I'm Feeling Lucky

Because you are a man. And men do not have periods. It's not your fault you don't have a heavy flow and a wide-set vagina.

Google

```
is jail |
is jail really that bad
is jail that bad
is jailbreaking illegal
is jail and prison the same thing
is jail effective
is jail fun
is jail bad
is jailbreaking legal
is jailbreaking safe
is jailbreaking your ipod bad
```

Google Search | I'm Feeling Lucky

A recent poll of inmates suggests that jail isn't really that bad. Four out of five felons say that they rather enjoy getting shanked in the yard, molested in the showers, the complete absence of women, and the really bad food. And, of course, they all love the free rent!

Google

```
god is p
god is perfect bible verse
god is perfect
god is patient
god is pooh bear
god is punishing haiti
god is personal
god is powerful
god is patient god is kind
god is peace
god is present
```

Google Search | I'm Feeling Lucky

A little known fact overlooked in most versions of the modern bible. Just imagine the shock of the recently deceased when they arrive at the pearly gates, only to find them being opened by St. Eeyore.

Google

```
i am going to d|
i am going to die
i am going to die alone
i am going to disneyland
i am going to die soon
i am going to die of boredom
i am going to die a virgin
i am going to disneyland lyrics
i am going to drink your milkshake
i am going to do a poo at paul's
i am going to drop a deuce on everybody
```

[Google Search] [I'm Feeling Lucky]

Let's just pray, for all of our safety and personal hygiene, that this was not typed into Google by Winnie the God Pooh.

Google

```
making a baby f|
making a baby from scratch
making a baby from pictures
making a baby free
making a baby face
making a baby for free
making a baby fleece blanket
```

[Google Search] [I'm Feeling Lucky]

Recipe courtesy of Julia Child: Add one penis to one ovulating vagina. Ejaculate.

Rinse. Lather. Repeat.

Google

```
a best|
a best friend is someone who
a best friend's job should be to immediately clear your computer history if you die
a best friend to set you right lyrics
a best friend quote
a best friend
a best kitchen
a best friend is someone quotes
a best web
a best friend song
a best friend is someone who quotes
```

[Google Search] [I'm Feeling Lucky]

I personally make all of my potential friends fill out an application and sign a release explicitly stating that they would be willing to send all photos of me wearing nothing but a sombrero with that donkey in Tijuana directly to the recycling bin in the event of my untimely death. Also, the blog under my pseudonym Bucky Naked detailing Tales of the She-Males must be deleted forever from the hard drive.

Google

```
why am i o|
why am i out of fertilizer in farmville
why am i obsessed with him
why am i obsessed with twilight
why am i overweight
why am i on google
why am i obsessed with food
why am i overeating
why am i obsessed with a girl
why am i obsessed with my ex
why am i on the internet
```

[Google Search] [I'm Feeling Lucky]

Funny how the Gods of Google subtly answer this question for Tubby. Look at the next three answers. Apparently, Slim Goodbody typed all four Whoogles in a row. Because you are on Google instead of jogging. Because you are obsessed with food. Because you overeat. Unfortunately, Two Ton Tillie did not query the more important fifth Whoogle, "Why am I not eating less and exercising rather than asking a computer to solve a simple problem for me?"

Google

satan cla|

santa claus
satan **claymation**
satan claus
satan claw
santa clara
mark twain satan **claymation**
blood on satan claw
blood on satan**'s** claw **soundtrack**
sons of satan clan

Google Search | I'm Feeling Lucky

You better watch out. Your soul's gonna fry. You're going to Hell, I'm telling you why. Satan Claus is coming to town.

Google

will a wal
will a walnut explode in pink lemonade

[Google Search] [I'm Feeling Lucky]

Yes. Massive explosion. Almost as massive as the explosion in your stomach if you drink a Coke whilst eating Pop Rocks.

Google

do pirat

do pirates **still exist**
do pirates **take baths**
do pirates **have a code of ethics**
do pirates **attack cruise ships**
do pirates **celebrate christmas**
do pirates **exist today**
do pirates **have tattoos**
do pirates **really exist**
do pirates **still exist today**
do pirates **wear bandanas**

| Google Search | I'm Feeling Lucky |

Because I have seen *Pirates of the Caribbean* (and been on the ride at Disney World), I now consider myself to be somewhat of an authority on all things pirate and plan to write a Wikipedia page. The "code" is more of a set of "guidelines" really.

Google

```
can i n
can i notarize a family member
can i notarize my son's signature
can i negotiate with credit card companies
can i notarize my husband's signature
can i network xp and windows 7
can i notarize my own documents
can i nurse while pregnant
can i network a mac and a pc
can i notarize in another state
can i name my child anything
```

[Google Search] [I'm Feeling Lucky]

Anything is a strange name for a child, but, to each his own. If vapid celebrities can name their kids Apple, Kal-El, and Moon Unit, then ordinary idiots can certainly name their little rugrat Anything Jones without fear of the kid growing up to get the shit kicked out of them every day on the playground.

Google

```
why cant co|
why cant cows walk down stairs
why cant cows go down stairs
why cant contour lines cross
why cant continents subduct
why cant collagen and elastin penetrate the skin
why cant college graduates find jobs
why cant connect to wireless
why can corn be digested
why cant covalent compounds conduct electricity
why cant communism work
```

[Google Search] [I'm Feeling Lucky]

They can, the lazy heifers just prefer to take the elevator. And, why is it that Google only cares about cows walking down stairs? I am more curious as to why they cannot walk up stairs. Come to think of it, maybe they can!

Google

```
what would happen if b|
what would happen if bees went extinct
what would happen if blood became too salty
what would happen if bacteria became extinct
what would happen if bees died
what would happen if black holes collide
what would happen if bacteria disappeared
what would happen if bella chose jacob
what would happen if betelgeuse exploded
what would happen if bees disappeared
what would happen if bees were extinct
```

[Google Search] [I'm Feeling Lucky]

The incidence of vampire heart disease would go through the roof.

Google

```
how to flirt|
how to flirt
how to flirt with a guy
how to flirt with a girl
how to flirt with a guy over text
how to flirt with a guy in middle school
how to flirt with a girl over text
how to flirt with your boyfriend
how to flirt with men
how to flirt with women
how to flirt online
```

[Google Search] [I'm Feeling Lucky]

Hang out at the mall and the Urban Outfitters where he shops. Do his homework for him. Offer to buy beer for him and his friends. And millions of other neat ideas included in the search results for how to become a pedophile.

Google

```
do men h
```

do men have periods
do men have **estrogen**
do men have **mammary glands**
do men have **pms**
do men have **hot flashes**
do men have **pregnancy symptoms**
do men have **thyroids**
do men have **menopause**
do men have **one less rib**
do men have **estrogen in their bodies**

[Google Search] [I'm Feeling Lucky]

Absolutely. Why else would pharmaceutical companies market a drug specifically for men called Flomax?

Google

how to get a pop
how to get a **popular guy** to **like you**
how to get a **popular girl** to **like you**
how to get a **popular guy** to **notice you**
how to get a **popular guy** to get **me pregnant**
how to get a **pop**tropica membership
how to get a **popular blog**
how to get a **popular girl** to **notice you**
how to get a **popular boy** to **like you**
how to get a **popular girl** to **be your friend**
how to get a pop **out player on myspace**

Google Search   I'm Feeling Lucky

Step 1: Join cheerleading team. Step 2: "Forget" to take birth control pills. Step 3: Giggle at everything he says. Step 4: Observe from over your growing stomach as he brags to his buddies about his uncanny ability to woo yet another teenage girl whose father never shows her enough affection.

Google

```
i wish di|
i wish disney movie
i wish digimon
i wish digimon lyrics
i wish diarrhea upon you
i wish digimon download
```

[Google Search] [I'm Feeling Lucky]

Wait a minute. For years I have been forced to resort to Ex Lax Brownies, Dulcolax Doughnuts, and Laxative Laced Lemon Pie to exact gastrointestinal revenge on my mortal enemies. If I had known I could simply wish diarrhea upon them, I would have saved myself thousands of man-hours in front of the oven.

Google

```
when jesus ca
when jesus came the corn mothers went away
when jesus came to jordan
when jesus came to harvard
when jesus came to birmingham
when jesus came to jordan lyrics
when jesus came into my heart
when jesus came to harvard summary
when jesus calms the storm
when jesus came into my heart lyrics
when jesus came into my life
```

Google Search   I'm Feeling Lucky

I, for one, am very appreciative of Jesus and his magical ability to remove those pesky corn mothers from society. Generally, it takes a high level of certain pesticides to eradicate those crazy ladies.

Google

```
i have a b
i have a big head and little arms
i have a balloon
i have a bad feeling about this
i have a big nose
i have a bump on my private
i have a bump on my labia
i have a bad case of diarrhea
i have a big head
i have a bump on my eyelid
i have a bump on my lip
```

[Google Search] [I'm Feeling Lucky]

Attention all paleontologists. We now have proof that Tyrannosaurus Rex was capable of using a computer keyboard, despite previous scientific hypotheses to the contrary.

Google

who decides the g|

who decides the **grammys**
who decides the **golden globes**
who decides the **gender of a baby**
who decides the **grammy winners**
who decides the **grammy awards**
who decides the **golden globe winners**
who decides the **gender of the baby**
who decides the **game of the year**

Google Search   I'm Feeling Lucky

Since 1987, the gender of all babies has been determined by Marcus Fillermore of Intercourse, Pennsylvania. Look it up on Yahoo if you don't believe me.

Google

```
i like to e|
i like to eat apples and bananas lyrics
i like to eat my skin
i like to eat apples and bananas
i like to eat eat eat apples and bananas lyrics
i like to eat poop
i like to eat ice cream and i really enjoy a nice pair of slacks
i like to eat
i like to eat eat eat
i like to eat apples and bananas chords
i like to eat sleep drink and be in love
```

[Google Search] [I'm Feeling Lucky]

This sounds like a bad Match.com profile. This tool is an ice cream loving, slacks wearing engineer whose hobbies include watching a lot of Star Trek and being socially awkward at any event involving more than one person.

Google

```
why is a ma|
why is a marathon 26.2 miles
why is a man whole cover round
why is a mac better than a pc
why is a mathematician like an airline
why is a marketing plan important
why is a marathon 26 miles
why is a marathon called a marathon
why is a marathon 26 miles and 385 yards
why is a mac better for graphic design
why is a marathon 26.2
```

[Google Search] [I'm Feeling Lucky]

Dear Secretary of Education: I know that times are tough. But, could you please reinstitute spelling classes in elementary school? Stop being such an asswhole and do it now! Yours truly, Kent Pack, Jackson Whole, Wyoming.

Google

```
i notice|
i noticed you noticing me
i notice lyrics automatic loveletter
i noticed how beautiful the sky was
i noticed how beautiful the sky was the other day
i noticed you're pretty gangster
i notice lyrics
i noticed that your gangster
i noticed that
i noticed your eyes are always glued to me lyrics
i noticed i was on fire
```

[Google Search] [I'm Feeling Lucky]

How do you "notice" you are on fire? Being on fire is not something you so nonchalantly recognize. Did Richard Pryor "notice" he was on fire after his freebase pipe exploded?

Google

does pooping m

does pooping make you lose weight
does pooping **make you skinnier**
does pooping **make you lose calories**

Google Search   I'm Feeling Lucky

Yes. Amoebic dysentery is all the new rage in weight loss.

Google

```
what does uri
what does urine taste like
what does urine contain
what does uri stand for
what does urine color mean
what does urine consist of
what does urine test check for
what does urinalysis test for
what does uri mean
what does uriel mean
what does urine smell like
```

[Google Search]   [I'm Feeling Lucky]

Surprisingly, it tastes like shit.

Google

```
jesus v

jesus vicente zambada-niebla
jesus verdejo
jesus vs frosty
jesus videos
jesus video
jesus valentine
jesus vs santa
jesus vegetarian
jesus venn diagram
jesus vs muhammad
```

Google Search   I'm Feeling Lucky

Who can forget the classic children's Christmas cartoon where the titular snowman and the son of God did battle in a steel cage match on MTV's *Celebrity Death Match*?

Google

how do you know if b
how do you know if **birth control fails**
how do you know if **breast milk has gone bad**
how do you know if **baby has dropped**
how do you know if **beef has gone bad**
how do you know if **bacon has gone bad**
how do you know if **buttermilk has gone bad**
how do you know if **baby is teething**
how do you know if **broccoli has gone bad**
how do you know if **blue cheese has gone bad**
how do you know if **birth control is working**

Google Search   I'm Feeling Lucky

If there is an infant preparing to make a swan dive out of your uterus, it is not working.

Google

seme
semester at sea
semen-based recipes
semester grade calculator
semester
semenya
semester hours
seme **uke quiz**
semele
seme **uke**
semester exam calculator

Google Search   I'm Feeling Lucky

Hey, don't knock it until you try it. The addition of protein never hurts, and most foods are not salted enough anyway.

Google

```
can i eat m|
can i eat mayonnaise while pregnant
can i eat mushrooms when pregnant
can i eat mozzarella when pregnant
can i eat mahi mahi while pregnant
can i eat moldy bread
can i eat mussels when pregnant
can i eat my own poop
can i eat moldy cheese
can i eat mussels while pregnant
can i eat mexican food while pregnant
```

[Google Search]   [I'm Feeling Lucky]

Soon we are probably going to see poop based recipes to go with the semen based recipes. This will be followed by a cookbook from the Shitfaced Contessa telling you all the ways to blend your bodily excretions and concoct them into a delightful casserole.

Google

i forgot w

i forgot what i was going to google
i forgot what **eight was for**
i forgot **when my last period was**
i forgot what **i was going to do**
i forgot **windows xp password**
i forgot what **i was fighting for lyrics**
i forgot what **it feels like to be normal**
i forgot what **email i used for xbox live**
i forgot what **i was going to look up**
i forgot what **i was looking for**

Google Search | I'm Feeling Lucky

This was the most common search during the Beta testing of Google when Reagan was in the White House.

Google

google is r
google is **redirecting me**
google is **retarded**
google is **redirecting**
google is **run by pigeons**
google is **run by aliens**
google is **redirected**
google is **ruining everything**
google is **really slow**
google is **rich**
google is **running slow**

Google Search | I'm Feeling Lucky

This explains the huge number of Whoogles dealing with poop.

Google

george bush is|
george bush is **a lizard**
george bush is **an idiot**
george bush**isms**
george bush is **a great president**
george bush is **the antichrist**
george bush is **our children learning**
george bush is **funny**
george bush is **the worst president ever**
george bush is **a nazi**
george bush is **a monkey**

Google Search   I'm Feeling Lucky

Most people do not remember that a pre-presidential W played the starring role, sans makeup, in *Jurassic Park 4*, which went straight to DVD.

Google

do clams p|

do clams **produce pearls**

do clams **poop**

how do clams **protect themselves**

how do clams **produce their shells**

how do clams **poop**

how do clams **procreate**

| Google Search | I'm Feeling Lucky |

Yes. Where do you think black pearls come from?

france is s|

france is **socialist**
france is **set to concede that it** is **aware of an alien presence on earth by no later than friday**
france is **surrounded by**
paris france is **southeast of the intersection of**
why france is **selling warships to russia**

Google Search | I'm Feeling Lucky

Of course they are. France concedes if you even look at it funny.

Just ask Germany.

Google

is it bad to e
is it bad to **eat late at night**
is it bad to **eat before bed**
is it bad to **eat** too **much fish**
is it bad to **eat boogers**
is it bad to **eat after working out**
is it bad to **exercise when you have a cold**
is it bad to **eat eggs everyday**
is it bad to **eat at night**
is it bad to **eat raw cookie dough**
is it bad to **eat snow**

Google Search	I'm Feeling Lucky

That depends on how old you are. Actually, I take that back. The only difference is that if you are four years old, your mother has to tell you it is bad to eat boogers. If you are old enough that you can type those six words correctly, you should not have to ask your mother, Google, or anybody else if it is bad.

Google

```
do unto|
do unto others bible verse
do unto others
do unto others as you would
do unto others scripture
do unto others as they do to you
do unto otters lesson plans
do unto others quote
do unto others wow
do unto otters
do unto others bible
```

Google Search   I'm Feeling Lucky

Apparently PETA is rewriting the Bible.

Google

i didnt know she

i **didn't** know she **was 3**

i didnt know she **had the gi joe kung fu grip**

i **didn't** know she **was 3 shirt**

i didnt know she **was 3**

Google Search | I'm Feeling Lucky

I will agree that finding a girl with the kung fu grip has always been the ultimate male fantasy according to *Soldier of Fortune* magazine. It takes happy endings to a whole new level, as long as you are into S&M.

Google

```
oprah u|
oprah unauthorized biography
oprah undercover boss
oprah uma
oprah upcoming shows
oprah upcoming guests
oprah underwear
oprah youtube
oprah undercover boss episode
oprah up in the air
oprah unauthorized
```

[Google Search] [I'm Feeling Lucky]

Even those of you out there with a panty fetish have to be a little bit turned off by this.

Google

```
why am i sm
```

why am i smart
why am i smarter than everyone
why am i smelling smoke all the time
why am i smelling ammonia
why am i smashing my hand with this hammer
why am i smelly
why am i small
why am i smelling cigarette smoke

Google Search   I'm Feeling Lucky

The hand eye coordination necessary to properly drive a nail into a piece of wood is severely diminished when you are also trying to type a ridiculous question into your computer at the same time.

Google

```
how is
how is babby formed
how is a raven like a writing desk
how is mrna made
how is hiv treated
how is a hurricane formed
how is hiv transmitted
how is carbon dating done
how is curling scored
how is tampa's climate affected by the gulf
how is vinegar made
```

[Google Search] [I'm Feeling Lucky]

I think the more relevant question here is, what is a babby?

New rule: if you don't know how to spell baby, and you don't know how babies are made, you are officially not allowed to procreate.

Google

can goo|

can google calendar sync with iphone
can good teaching be learned
can goods
can god exist without evil
can google calendar sync with ical
can good teaching be taught
can google voice receive mms
can google hear me
can google calendar sync with outlook
can goods shelf life

Google Search   I'm Feeling Lucky

Why don't you ask Google verbally instead of typing this question in and find out?

Google

```
floppy fa
floppy fail 40
floppy farting hippo
floppy face syndrome
floppy facebook
floppy fanny
floppy fan
format floppy fat32
linux format floppy fat
```

[Google Search] [I'm Feeling Lucky]

This Whoogle comes up as you start to type in "Kirstie Alley."

Google

when i eat
when i eat **my stomach hurts**
when i eat i **feel nauseous**
when i eat **my stomach swells**
when i eat i **feel sick**
when i eat **my chest hurts**
when i eat i **get tired**
when i eat i **feel bloated**
when i eat i **get dizzy**
when i eat **hot cheetos i get crazy**
when i eat i **get diarrhea**

[Google Search] [I'm Feeling Lucky]

Who eats Cheetos, much less hot Cheetos? And is this actually asking a question, or some inexplicable desire to tell Google about yourself to make the relationship less one-sided?

Google

```
if me
if men were angels
if men could menstruate
if memory serves
if meaning
if men wrote advice columns
if men could talk
if men had periods
if member
if men ruled the world
if me.dirty then me.dirty false
```

Google Search   I'm Feeling Lucky

If men could menstruate, tampons would probably be the less favored way of dealing with Uncle Flo.

Google

```
would you sa
would you say i have a plethora of pinatas
would you say he's just a friend
would you save my soul tonight
would you say i told you so lyrics
would you say he's just a friend lyrics
would you say i have a plethora of gifts
would you say i told you so
would you say lyrics
would you say thank you if i spank you lyrics
would you save me lyrics
```

            [Google Search]   [I'm Feeling Lucky]

No. I would say you have an overabundance of piñatas. Or
perhaps a glut of piñatas. But a plethora? Not so much.

Google

why am i ru

why am i **running out of hot water**
why am i **running slower**
why am i **running a fever**
why am i **running for office**
why am i **rude**
why am i **run down**
why am i **running and not losing weight**
why am i **running out of disk space**
why am i **rubbish at maths**

Google Search   I'm Feeling Lucky

This Whoogle was undoubtedly followed by the same Einstein asking Google, "Why am I garbage at Englishes" right before submitting his 400 overall SAT score to the local community college.

Google

when i grow up i
when i grow up i **want to be like mommy**
when i grow up i **wanna be famous lyrics**
when i grow up i **want to be**
when i grow up i **want to be a notorious homosexual**
when i grow up i **want to be an old woman**
when i grow up i **want to be a principal or a caterpillar**
when i grow up i **wanna be famous**
when i grow up i **want to be a forester**
when i grow up i **want to be like mommy snopes**
when i grow up i **want to be like mommy shovel**

Google Search   I'm Feeling Lucky

Who can blame little Mary for aspiring to such great heights? One
day, after many years of schooling and study, she can use her
degree to operate her own educational facility or to build a cocoon
around herself and hang precariously from a tree.

Google

```
my wife le
my wife left me
my wife left me what do i do
my wife left town with a banana
my wife left me for a guy named jesus
my wife left me for another woman
my wife left me for a woman
my wife left me for jesus
my wife let herself go
my wife left with the kids
my wife left me and wont talk to me
```

    Google Search   I'm Feeling Lucky

A cucumber? That I could see. A salami? No problem there.

But being kicked to the curb for a banana is just plain bad taste.

Unless, of course, it was split in two with a couple of scoops of ice

cream and some hot fudge.

Google

```
i do not like m
i do not like my big red wife
i do not like my husband
i do not like myself
i do not like my job
i do not like my mother in law
i do not like my husband anymore
i do not like my mother
i do not like my child
i do not like my mittens
i do not like my state of mind
```

| Google Search | I'm Feeling Lucky |

The Jolly Green Giant was heard to espouse this lament.
Apparently, Big Red is not so enamored with the Jolly Green one,
either, and says that he is not actually giant, if you know what I
mean.

Google

```
france is|
france islands
france is the size of what u.s. state
france issues
france islam
france is known for
france is famous for
france is a country i didn't know that
france is in what country
france is my favorite city
france isd code
```

Google Search   I'm Feeling Lucky

It turns out that there are a lot of things I didn't know about culture and geography, despite gradumacating from an American high school. For example, I didn't know that North America was a continent. Or that there are, in fact, seven continents on the planet. I might be able to point out the United States on a map. But it would probably be better if we didn't bet any money on it.

Google

is there an o
is there an owl on the one dollar bill
is there an official language in the united states
is there an over the counter medicine for pink eye
is there an over the counter medicine for uti
is there an online pokemon game
is there an old zealand
is there an official eclipse trailer
is there an outback steakhouse in australia
is there an online sims game
is there an online game like the sims

Google Search   I'm Feeling Lucky

Yes, the GPS I bought at the flea market for $9.95 tells me it is right between Old Hampshire and Old Jersey.

Google

farting in a

farting in a **jar**
farting in an **elevator**
farting in a **space suit**
farting in a **wetsuit**
farting in a **relationship**
farting in a **library**
farting in a **hot tub**
farting in **anime**

Google Search | I'm Feeling Lucky

NASA, 1968. Afraid to ask his superiors in Houston about the possible effect of odor that would emanate around the lunar module should the Tang and Beans supper have negative effects later in the journey, Neil Armstrong turns to the beta version of Google for answers. Rocket science can be tricky.

Google

ever wonder why
ever wonder why
ever wonder why **jokes**
ever wonder why **questions**
ever wonder why **quotes**
ever wonder why **humor**
ever wonder why **lyrics**
ever wonder why **lyrics ryan bingham**
ever wonder why **ice cubes are so boring**
ever wonder why **chords**
ever wonder why **sayings**

Google Search   I'm Feeling Lucky

Usually I find that it is a waste of time to contemplate the fun factor of frozen water. Solution: drown them in vodka, and contemplate something more meaningful, like the meaning of life or whether it is possible for a dog to get a woman pregnant.

Google

```
how many sh|
how many shrek movies are there
how many shots in a fifth
how many mushrooms to take first time
how many shots in a handle
how many shots in a 750ml bottle
how many sheets of paper for one stamp
how many shuttle launches left
how many shamu's have there been
how many shingles in a bundle
how many shots to get drunk
```

[Google Search] [I'm Feeling Lucky]

We could go in depth to the exact number of shots, but a quicker response would be: not enough to get any self-respecting bum drunk.

Google

is it legal to pa|

is it legal to **park in front of someone's house**
is it legal to **pass on the right**
is it legal to pay **in pennies**
is it legal to **pass out flyers**
is it legal to **paint your license plate**
is it legal to **park in front of a mailbox**
is it legal to **park in front of your own driveway**
is it legal to **pass a school bus**
is it legal to pay **less than minimum wage**
is it legal to **park a trailer on the road**

Google Search | I'm Feeling Lucky

Of course it is legal. However, if you pull this maneuver, it is also legal for the cashier to flick them back at you one at a time in the hopes that his many attempts resulting from your $2 purchase will cause some serious injuries, for which he cannot be held liable.

Google

```
is bp |
```

is bp **an american company**
is bp **insured**
is bp **a good buy**
is bp **a buy**
is bp **dividend safe**
is bp **gas better**
is bp **responsible**
is bp **gas good**
is bp **to blame**
is bp **a good stock**

[Google Search] [I'm Feeling Lucky]

In a Gallup poll of 1,000 Louisiana Gulf Coast pelicans, 98 percent said "no" and 2 percent were unable to respond to the poll taker since their mouths were glued shut by tar balls.

Google

```
does la|
does lady gaga have a weiner
does lady gaga have man parts
does lady gaga have a willy
does lady gaga smoke
does lady gaga have balls
does lady gaga have kids
does lady gaga wear a wig
does laura bush smoke
does latisse really work
does latisse work
```

[Google Search] [I'm Feeling Lucky]

No. But she does have an Alejandro. And a Roberto. I am so embarrassed that I know the answer to that one.

Google

```
i am going to g|
i am going to get fired
i am going to go in spanish
i am going to grape you
i am going to get you
i am going to go
i am going to grammar
i am going to get married
i am going to go in french
i am going to go to bed
i am going to go grammar
```

[Google Search] [I'm Feeling Lucky]

I hate being graped. The concept of being graped sends shivers down my spine. I will do almost anything for you, but if you insist on administering a good, old fashioned graping to me, you will need to be sure I am very drunk first.

Google

is afghanistan in
is afghanistan in **the middle east**
is afghanistan in **asia**
is afghanistan in **europe**
is afghanistan in **southwest asia**
is afghanistan in **iraq**
is afghanistan in **africa**
is afghanistan in **the winter olympics**
is afghanistan in **central asia**
is afghanistan in **southeast asia**
is afghanistan in **asia or europe**

Google Search   I'm Feeling Lucky

I would be less frightened by this question if I did not trace the IP address back to the White House.

Google

can pigs e
can pigs eat **humans**
can pigs eat **chocolate**
can pigs eat **meat**
can pigs eat **bones**
can pigs eat **bacon**
can pigs eat **hay**
can pigs eat **pork**
can pigs eat **acorns**
can pigs eat **people**
can pigs eat **chicken bones**

> Google Search   I'm Feeling Lucky

Pigs love to eat humans. Baby back ribs have a whole different meaning at the swine version of Chili's. And don't even ask us about the kind of bacon Porky likes to fry up for breakfast.

Google

```
is it ga|
```

is it gage **or** gauge
is it gas **or a heart attack**
is it gas **or am i pregnant**
is it gas **or the baby moving**
is it gandhi **or ghandi**
is it gaga **or gaga**
is it gas **or appendicitis**
is it ganesh **or ganesha**
is it gambia **or the gambia**
is it game **over for the console**

| Google Search | I'm Feeling Lucky |

To the gods of Google: please tell me, is it gas or am I pregnant?
I hate it when I can't tell whether I'm spawning new life, in the
throes of death . . . or maybe it was just that Mexican food I had
for lunch?

Google

```
why are m

why are michael jackson's kids white
why are my hands always cold
why are men attracted to breasts
why are me
why are my feet always cold
why are man whole covers round
why are my cigarettes going out
why are my nipples sore
why are manatees endangered
why are my cookies flat

        [Google Search]  [I'm Feeling Lucky]
```

Stop typing this inquiry to Google, and take a quick look downward. See those two shiny new hoop earrings that were not attached to your areola before you decided that doing ten Patron shots was a good idea last night? Don't worry, I think the Piercing Pagoda has a decent return policy, and some Neosporin waiting for you.

Google

i dont like a|

i dont like **anyone lyrics**
i dont like **anyone**
i dont like **anything**
i dont like **anyone but you lyrics**
i dont like **alcohol**
i dont like **avatar**
i dont like **any of my friends**
i dont like **anything about myself**
i dont like **asians**
i dont like **americans**

[Google Search] [I'm Feeling Lucky]

Somebody needs to Google the definition of the term "friends."

Google

```
god g
god grant me the serenity prayer
god grant me the serenity
god grew tired of us
god games
god grant me the serenity quote
god gold and glory
god gave rock and roll to you
god give me the serenity
god gave me you dave barnes lyrics
god gene
```

[Google Search] [I'm Feeling Lucky]

Taking on God in Scrabble is a nightmare. You can't even begin to question Him on a word, or He will insist that "ZQKJW" is most certainly a word because He is all knowing and will claim He just created it, even though it is not in the dictionary.

Google

what is it called when a

what is it called when a **word** is **spelled the same backwards**
what is it called when a **giraffe swallowed a toy jet**
what is it called when a **change** is **made in the constitution**
what is it called when an **atom gets charged**
what is it called when a **sea bird lands on a channel marker**
what is it called when a **pirate** is **left in a cage to die and left there**
what is it called when a **gas turns into a liquid**
what is it called when a **liquid turns into a gas**
what is it called when a **man gets fixed**
what is it called when a **solid turns into a gas**

Google Search   I'm Feeling Lucky

Apparently pirates are routinely left to die twice in the same sentence.

Google

why am i i
why am i **itching down below**
why am i **important to my family**
why am i **interested in this position**
why am i **in the water and wtf is that**
why am i **itching all over**
why am i **itchy**
why am i **insecure**
why am i **itching all over my body**
why am i **in college**
why am i **insecure in my relationship**

Google Search   I'm Feeling Lucky

Your laptop is also wondering why you are in the water and how you got an Internet connection while you are swimming. To answer the second part of your brilliant query, "that" is a current of 10,000 volts of pure, unadulterated electricity about to enter your body and fry you like a death row inmate after twenty years of appeals.

Google

```
why is my po|
```

why is my po**op green**
why is my po**op black**
why is my po**op white**
why is my po**op blue**
why is my po**op orange**
why is my po**op bloody**
why is my po**op yellow**
why is my po**op red**
why is my po**op bright green**
why is my po**op dark green**

[Google Search] [I'm Feeling Lucky]

Unlike Skittles, this is a rainbow you probably don't want to taste.

Google

```
do gin
do gingers have souls
do ginger people have ginger pubes
do gingers feel more pain
do ginny pigs bite
do gingers go grey
do ginny and harry get married
do gingers have no soul
do gingers
do gingers have soles
do ginger people smell
```

| Google Search | I'm Feeling Lucky |

Ginger people? The only ginger person I am aware of is the Gingerbread Man, and I am pretty sure that the epic children's story was not illustrated with pubes even if the cookies were naked and running from the animals. Just like Barbie and Ken have no cash and prizes, ginger people are also androgynous and the fire crotch is left to your imagination.

Google

the bed

the bedford reader 10th edition
the bedroom store
the bedford incident
the bedford reader 9th edition
the bedwetting store
the bedford handbook
the bed is undefiled
the bed restaurant in miami
the bed is on fire with passion and love
the bedford reader

[Google Search] [I'm Feeling Lucky]

Are you sick of having your children sleep soundly and wake up with dry sheets and clean pajamas? Tired of hearing your friends brag about their sons and daughters who piss all over themselves mid-slumber? Well, be sick and tired no more, come to the bedwetting store! We have all the products needed to make sure your child urinates freely all night, so you can spend countless hours making sure your kid's room does not smell like a construction site Port-o-Potty.

Google

```
can a do|
can a dog get a woman pregnant
can a dog get a cold
can a dog be spayed while in heat
can a dog get the flu
can a dog get pregnant when not in heat
can a dog get swine flu
can a dog break its tail
can a dog take aspirin
can a dog catch a cold
can a dog take benadryl
```

[Google Search]   [I'm Feeling Lucky]

Certainly. It can happen for two reasons. First, male dogs are notoriously bad at remembering to use birth control. Second, even if they do remember, dogs have trouble putting on a condom because they do not have opposable thumbs.

Google

```
gummi bears a|
gummi bears and vodka
gummi bears acapella
gummi bears a new beginning
gummi bears amazon
gummi bears and water
gummi bears adventures
gummi bears animation
```

[Google Search] [I'm Feeling Lucky]

"Gummis and Goose" is the hottest panty dropper in all of third grade.

Google

honestly i w
honestly i **was never that hungry hungry**

Google Search	I'm Feeling Lucky

I was, however, always that thirsty thirsty. So I drank a Gummis and Goose Goose. Make that a double.

Google

```
i like to eat p|
```

i like to eat **poop**
i like to eat **pie**
i like to eat **pancakes**
i like to eat **people from other planets especially yall**
i like to eat **pepperoni pizza song**
i like to eat **paper**
i like to eat **people**

[Google Search] [I'm Feeling Lucky]

Dear Arkansas: other states are not planets.

Google

bat po|

bat poop
bat poop **in mascara**
bat**pod**
bat **poems**
bat poop **coffee**
bat poop **in doritos**
bat po**ison**
bat po**kemon**
bat po**llination**
bat **poems for kids**

Google Search | I'm Feeling Lucky

Leave it to those wonderful chefs at Frito Lay to find the magical ingredient that all other snack manufacturers missed.

Google

speak af|

speak af**rikaans**
speak af**rica**
speak af**rican language**
how to speak african
learn to speak afrikaans
how to speak african language
how to speak afghanistan
how to speak african click
learn to speak african
where do they speak afrikaans

Google Search   I'm Feeling Lucky

African is generally considered to be the fourth most widely spoken language in the world, preceded by American, European, and Asian.

Google

do you really h|

do you really **have to pee in a girl's mouth to make babies**
do you really **have the stamina lyrics**
do you really **have to pay taxes**
do you really **have a global strategy**
do you really **have to pay for facebook**
do you really **have to warm up** your **car**
do you really **have to dry clean**
do you really **have stamina**
do you really **have the stamina kanye**
do you really **hurt me lyrics**

Google Search I'm Feeling Lucky

Mom, where do babies come from? Well, honey, stories of storks and intercourse being the source of babies are actually both just urban myths. The truth is that sperm comes from urine, and is only able to get to a woman's egg through oral ingestion. Forget the birds and the bees, folks. From now on it's all about waterfalls and caves.

Google

i wish i was w
i wish i was **white**
i wish i was **were**
i wish i was **with you quotes**
i wish i was **with you poems**
i wish i was **with you lyrics**
i wish i was **were grammar**
i wish i was **where** i was **when** i was wishing i was **here**
i wish i was **with you tonight**
i wish i was **with you in spanish**
i wish i was **wrong lyrics**

Google Search   I'm Feeling Lucky

This is proof positive that Michael Jackson used Google as his search engine.

Google

am i ch

am i **chubby quiz**

am i **cheating**

am i **cheating on my boyfriend quiz**

am i **cherokee**

am i **charming quiz**

am i **charismatic quiz**

am i **christian or catholic**

am i **cheap**

am i **charismatic**

am i **cheating quiz**

Google Search   I'm Feeling Lucky

You would think that this would be a simple question that one might be able to figure out without Google's assistance. But, you would be wrong. Luckily, Google has 244,000 search results for quizzes to help you to determine whether you are cheating on your man. I mined through the results and came up with my own one question quiz to help girls sort out their conundrums: Did you do something with another guy or girl who was not your boyfriend? If you answered "yes," you can go ahead and start Googling the more colorful terms used to describe big ol' cheaters.

Google

```
my bre|
my breast friend
my breast milk is decreasing
my breasts are sore
my bread
my breasts hurt
my brest friend vs boppy
my breast are sore what does that mean
my breasts are getting bigger
my brest friend slipcover
my breath smells like poo
```

[Google Search] [I'm Feeling Lucky]

Shocker here, but your boyfriend isn't nearly as distraught over this concern as you are.

Google

if i make 4
if i make **40000 a year how much is that an hour**

Google Search | I'm Feeling Lucky

If you have to ask this question to Google, instead of using a calculator, the simple answer is . . . minimum wage. Or less.

Google

poop v
poop **video**
poop **vacuum**
poop **videos on youtube**
poop**ville**
poop **valhalla**
poop **vomit**
poop **vs pee**
poop **vector**
poop **video games**
poop **vein in shrimp**

Google Search | I'm Feeling Lucky

Again, I am confused. Is this Whoogle the result of some senior citizen with dementia who is confused about the blending of colors in their Depends? Or a *South Park* episode I missed commemorating a UFC showdown of bodily excretions?

Google

```
why is there
why is there a dead pakistani on my couch
why is there fuzz on a tennis ball
why is there a worm in tequila
why is there an apple on the cover of twilight
why is there no j street in dc
why is there two l's in google
why is there blood in my stool
why is there a barcode on google
why is there a circle around the moon
why is there daylight savings time
```

Google Search   I'm Feeling Lucky

First things first. The question should be, why **are** there two L's in Google, not, why is there? And apparently I am missing something here. . . .

Google

my cow|

my cowboy lyrics
my cow **is a lovely helicopter**
my cowboy music video
my coworkers don't like me
my cowboy jessie james video
my coworker is an idiot
my coworker hates me
my coworker is a slacker
my coworker smells
my cowboy jessie james mediafire

Google Search | I'm Feeling Lucky

Rural farm kids with Internet access are proving that acid is no longer a drug exclusively for the use of teenagers at raves. We are anxious to see what form the already enigmatic sport of cow tipping takes in this state of delirium.

Google

```
do girls g
do girls get boners
do girls get turned on
do girls get loose
do girls get pleasure from tampons
do girls get circumcised
do girls grow after menstruation
do girls go commando
do girls get morning wood
do girls give guys hickies
do girls give guys promise rings
```

[Google Search]   [I'm Feeling Lucky]

Why do you think girls cross their legs? Obviously it is to hide those massive hard-ons that are just as embarrassing for the fairer sex.

Google

```
i used my |
i used my grandma as a skateboard
i used my mom's credit card
i used my parents credit card
i used my mom's vibrator
i used my imagination
```

Google Search   I'm Feeling Lucky

It was honestly not bad like you think though. I just needed something to scramble the eggs so I could bring her breakfast in bed. Besides, I washed it for her when I was finished.

Google

```
poor pl
```

poor places **lyrics**
poor planning on your part does not constitute an emergency on my part
poor play **uldum**
poor **pluto**
poor places **chords**
poor planning on your part **poster**
poor planning **quote**
poor places **tab**
poor pluto **book**
poor places **wilco lyrics**

[Google Search] [I'm Feeling Lucky]

This only goes for you though. Because, contrarily, if I choose to procrastinate, you had better act like there is a fire when I need something done.

Google

satan b

satan **bible**
satan **burger**
satan **bible verses**
satan **band**
satan **bite the dust**
satan **bite the dust lyrics**
satan **beer**
satan **before the fall**
satan **being cast out of heaven**
satan **bug**

Google Search   I'm Feeling Lucky

Sometimes, there is nothing better than pulling up to the drive through at McDevils and ordering one of these bad boys. But, I hate those damned commercials where that evil clown Lonnie McLucifer tries to convince children to order an Unhappy Meal just to get the cheap toy pitchfork.

Google

```
fish rid|
```

fish ri**ddles**
fish ri**ding a bicycle**
fish ri**de bicycles**
fish ri**de bicycles release date**
fish ri**ding bicycle**
fish ri**ding a bike**
fish ri**ddle the hobbit**
fish ri**dgefield wa**
fish ri**ddle hobbit**
fish ri**der**

[Google Search] [I'm Feeling Lucky]

Fish have no business riding bicycles. It is inherently dangerous
for them, as they have no legs or feet, so peddling is difficult if
not impossible. I may start a movement to have a law passed
that, because of this danger, fish must wear a helmet in order to
Schwinn rather than swim.

what does it mean when i|

what does it mean when it **burns** when **you pee**
what does it mean when it **hurts to pee**
what does it mean when i **dream about my teeth falling out**
what does it mean when it **hurts to swallow**
what does it mean when i **dream about being pregnant**
what does it mean when it **hurts to poop**
what does it mean when it **rains on your wedding day**
what does it mean when i **dream about my boyfriend cheating on me**
what does it mean when i **dream about my crush**
what does it mean when i **dream about my ex**

Google Search   I'm Feeling Lucky

It means that you probably should have worn a condom.

Google

why can't gh
why can't ghosts **have babies**
why can't ghosts **cross water**

Google Search   I'm Feeling Lucky

Ghosts cannot have babies because their transcendent properties make it difficult for ghostly sperm to stay inside of ghostly uteri. This is similar to how gravity prevents conception if you have sex when you are standing up. For every seemingly silly Whoogle, there is a simple, scientific explanation.

Google

can monk|

can monkeys **swim**
can monkeys **talk**
can monkeys **cry**
can monk**s marry**
can monkeys **be pets**
can monkeys **fly**
can monkeys **smoke weed**
can monkeys **get aids**
can monkeys **laugh**
can monkeys **and humans mate**

[Google Search] [I'm Feeling Lucky]

Yes, and the majority of Ebola researchers agree that monkeys smoking weed is pretty harmless. It's when your monkey gets into the harder drugs and goes more spastic than usual that you should become concerned.

Google

poop f|

poop **facts**
poop **floats**
poop **freeze**
poop **from there**
poop **floating or sinking**
poop **floating**
poop **floats dr oz**
poop **face**
poop **for sale**
poop **font**

[Google Search] [I'm Feeling Lucky]

Any bidders? Shop around and compare! Lower prices than eBay!
And, for you nice lady, we will throw in a free colostomy bag so
you can carry your shit home without fear of breakage.

Google

i'd like to c
i'd like to **check you for ticks**
i'd like to **corinne bailey rae lyrics**
i'd like to **change the world lyrics**
i'd like to **call it beauty**
i'd like to **call it beauty lyrics**
i'd like to **change the world**
i'd like to **corinne bailey rae**
i'd like to **cut your head off so i can weigh it**
i'd like to **change the world tab**
i'd like to **call it beauty corinne bailey rae lyrics**

Google Search   I'm Feeling Lucky

After I am finished weighing it, I will probably dice up the remainder of your parts and sell them piecemeal to Hannibal Lecter to enjoy with some fava beans and a nice Chianti.

Google

```
can i use ba
can i use baby shampoo on my dog
can i use baby oil as lube
can i use baby shampoo on my puppy
can i use baby wipes on my dog
can i use band hero with rockband
can i use baking powder instead of yeast
can i use bacitracin on my dog
can i use baby carrots for baby food
can i use baby powder on my dog
can i use baking powder instead of cornstarch
```

[Google Search] [I'm Feeling Lucky]

The grand majority of Americans can't seem to be bothered to even pick up after their mutts when they crap in the park. But apparently there is the other extreme: those people who not only clean up after their dog, but also make sure that all fecal matter is wiped clean before the dog starts licking its balls again. Is your dog too good for generic? Worried about chafing its bum hole with Charmin? Not to worry, Huggies are ideal for your pup too.

Google

fun ways to t
fun ways to **teach vocabulary**
fun ways to **teach multiplication**
fun ways to **tell family you're pregnant**
fun ways to **teach grammar**
fun ways to **teach division**
fun ways to **teach math**
fun ways to **teach fractions**
fun ways to **teach spelling**
fun ways to **tell people you're pregnant**
fun ways to **teach sight words**

[Google Search] [I'm Feeling Lucky]

The most fun way to go about this would be to leave a receipt from Planned Parenthood on the counter.

Google

is chica
is chicago **illinois located on a bay**
is chicago **a good place to live**
is chicago **a state**
is chicago **central time**
is chicago is **not** chicago
is chicago is **not** chicago **lyrics**
is chicago **dangerous**
is chicago **a state or city**
is chicago **safe**
is chicago **airport closed**

[Google Search] [I'm Feeling Lucky]

Neither. Chicago is a town. My kind of town, Chicago is.

Google

tape my thumb
tape my thumb**s to my hands**
i want to tape my thumbs
i'd like to tape my thumbs
i would like to tape my thumbs **to my hands to see what it would be like to be a dinosaur**
how to tape my thumb
how do i tape my thumb

Google Search   I'm Feeling Lucky

Um . . . sometimes, it is best to just let these Whoogles stand on their own.

Google

poop ca

poop **cake**
poop **cartoons**
poop cake **recipe**
poop **calendar**
poop c**andy**
poop **catcher game**
poop **calculator**
poop catcher
pop cap
poop c**auses pink eye**

Google Search | I'm Feeling Lucky

Make a memo to all the online translators . . . in English, we call
Mr. Crapper's novel invention a "toilet."

what if my s

| what if my **social security number is stolen** |
| what if my **spouse declares bankruptcy** |
| what if my **spouse has bad credit** |
| what if my **sperm is yellow** |
| what if my **snot is yellow** |
| what if my **social security card is stolen** |
| what if my **sperm is clear** |
| what if my **stool is black** |
| what if my **snowboard is too short** |
| what if my **spleen hurts** |

Google Search   I'm Feeling Lucky

Prepare to be the proud papa of a jaundiced junior.

Google

i can count t
i can count **to potato**
i can count **to schfifty five**
i can count **to potato meme**
i can count **to 55**
i can count **to potato retard**
i can count **the ones i love on both hands**
i can count **to 100 certificate**
i can count **to potato the ringer**
i can count **to sausage**
i can count **to purple backwards**

Google Search | I'm Feeling Lucky

Great. Now, since you think you're so smart, tell me the product of fuchsia times cerulean.

Google

```
does fart
does farting burn calories
does fart powder work
does farting mean your healthy
does fart candy work
does farting pollute the air
does farting break wudu
does farting contribute to global warming
does farting spread germs
does farting cause global warming
does fat burn
```

[Google Search]   [I'm Feeling Lucky]

Yes, another inconvenient truth. Al Gore will soon start campaign-ing for a worldwide ban on beans.

Google

disguise mys
> **disguise mys**elf as a sleeping pill
> **robots in** disguise my**space**
> **masters of** disguise my**space**
> **silent** disguise my**space**

[Google Search] [I'm Feeling Lucky]

This is a little game I like to call "going rogue as a roofie." Endless fun to be had at many a swanky club.

Google

```
do fat p|
```

do fat **people fart more**
do fat **people cause global warming**
do fat **people have more blood**
do fat **people stay warmer**
do fat **people burn more calories**
do fat **people smell**
do fat **people poop more**
do fat **people lose weight faster**
do fat **people sweat more**
do fat **people float**

Google Search   I'm Feeling Lucky

Obviously, yes. Why do you think you never hear of fat people dying in drowning accidents?

Google

```
can you get pregnant from o|
can you get pregnant from outercourse
can you get pregnant from one time
```

[Google Search] [I'm Feeling Lucky]

Silly question. Everybody knows that it takes at least 750 million sperm, or three "full blown" intercourse sessions, to fertilize an egg. Thanks, science!

Google

is it normal to have f

is it normal to have **feelings for someone else**
is it normal to have **fever during pregnancy**
is it normal to have **frequent headaches during pregnancy**
is it normal to have **floaters**
is it normal to have **fat rolls**
is it normal to have **foamy urine**
is it normal to have **fights in a relationship**

Google Search | I'm Feeling Lucky

Only if you mistook the dishwashing liquid for your evening cocktail.

Google

```
making a chair
```

```
making a chair cushion
making a chair cover
making a chair from a tree
making a chair slipcover
making a chair out of cardboard
making a chair seat
making a chair rail
making a chair into a glider
making a chair pad
making a chair out of newspaper
```

[Google Search] [I'm Feeling Lucky]

Gone are the days where newspapers were only good for day old news, wrapping fish, and lining birdcages. Now, with just a few folds, a nail here and there, and some of Elmer's finest, you can make a delightful recliner that will put La-Z-Boy to shame. Just don't sit on it with your white pants.

Google

i accidentally p
i accidentally **put diesel in my car**
i accidentally **put in two tampons**
i accidentally **pooped my pants**
i accidentally **picked a mole**
i accidentally **poked someone on facebook**
i accidentally **popped a pimple**
i accidentally **pulled out my eyelashes**

[Google Search] [I'm Feeling Lucky]

This Whoogle raises the obvious companion question: Does anyone purposely poop their pants?

Google

is it true that d|

is it true that **dogs** mouths are cleaner than humans
is it true that **dogs see in black and white**
is it true that **demi lovato cuts herself**
is it true that **daddy yankee burned the mexican flag**
is it true that **dogs cant eat chocolate**
is it true that **dna**
is it true that **daddy long legs are poisonous**
is it true that **dogs are used as shark bait**
is it true that **dogs can only see black and white**
is it true that **dogs can see ghosts**

Google Search | I'm Feeling Lucky

I have always wondered this myself. I went straight to the source, and asked Fido. His surprising response? Silence. I somehow forgot that although dogs can speak English, they choose not to. However, he did slobber on me and then ran off and shit on the carpet, so I am assuming his answer was no.

Google

```
why is ur|
why is urban meyer stepping down
why is urine yellow
why is urban meyer leaving
why is uranus blue
why is uranus tilted
why is urine cloudy
why is urine called pee
why is uranus called uranus
why is urban meyer resigning
why is urine yellow after taking vitamins
```

[Google Search] [I'm Feeling Lucky]

Because it is 20 degrees out here and I have been sitting in the freezing cold waiting for you! So stop asking so many questions about my anus.